Travel Book:

A Travel Guide Of Hidden Gems That Takes You On A Journey

Bill Rogers

© 2018

Thanks for your purchase.

We also recommend that you get

"Surprising and Shocking Fun Facts:
The Treasure Book of Amazing Trivia"
by to compliment this book.

You can purchase it on this Link:
https://www.amazon.com/dp/B07D6
QJ7H1

COPYRIGHT

Travel Book: A Travel Guide Of Hidden Gems That Takes You On A Journey

By Bill Rogers

Copyright @2018 By Bill Rogers

All Rights Reserved.

This declaration is deemed fair and valid by both the American Bar Association and the Committee of Publishers Association and is legally binding throughout the United States.

Furthermore, the transmission, duplication or reproduction of any of the following work, including precise information, will be considered an illegal act, irrespective whether it is done electronically or in print. The legality extends to creating a secondary or tertiary copy of the work or a recorded copy and is only allowed with express written consent of the Publisher. All additional rights are reserved.

The information in the following pages is broadly considered to be a truthful and accurate account of facts, and as such any inattention, use or misuse of the information in question by the reader will render any resulting actions solely under their purview. There are no scenarios in which the publisher or the original author of this work can be in any fashion deemed liable for any hardship or damages that may befall them after undertaking information described herein.

Additionally, the information found on the following pages is intended for informational purposes only and should thus be considered, universal. As befitting its nature, the information presented is without assurance regarding its continued validity or interim quality. Trademarks that mentioned are done without written consent and can in no way be considered an endorsement from the trademark holder.

TABLE OF CONTENTS

Festivals

The Belgian carnivals

Carnival is a great celebration anywhere, and of course everyone knows the carnivals in Rio and Venice - but Belgium has its own breed of carnival, crazier and considerably more boozy than most.

At Binche, the carnival celebrations span three days. The first day has a parade of marching bands and fancy dress, each of the carnival associations marching together. The second day is for the children, dressed up as Harlequins or Pierrots, and barrel-organ players wander the streets, playing for dances as they go. But it's the third day, Shrove Tuesday, which is the climax of the celebrations and which is unique to Binche.

It starts as early as four in the morning, as the first 'Gilles' start their march from outlying farms and suburban houses into the town center. A clarinet plays a mournful little tune and a snare drum snaps a sharp rhythm, but as the Gilles call on house after house to collect their comrades, it's the sound of marching feet in wooden clogs on the cobbles that fills the air. By the time most people are about, the Gilles are all in town, having their tenth or eleventh glass of champagne and eating smoked salmon for their breakfast.

Now you get to see them en masse, and it's a frightening sight; they're like giants, their uniforms decorated with Belgian flags and heraldic symbols, and their faces covered with identical masks. Every Gille has green glass spectacles; every Gille has a tightly curled mustache. When they march, it's like watching an army of clones. When they reach the main square, they spread out into a circle, and dance, shuffling in their wooden clogs; and then it's time for lunch in the town hall.

In the afternoon, the masks have gone, and instead, the Gilles wear immense tall hats of ostrich feathers which sway as they walk. They parade on the main street, throwing blood oranges to the passers-by - if you catch enough, they make very good marmalade. And the carnival ends, eventually, with fireworks in the town square - though for some, carnival continues in the pubs and bars of the town until the early hours.

If you can't get to Binche, but you can visit Brussels on Shrove Tuesday, you'll see the Mannekin Pis put on his Gilles costume - with his basket of oranges.

Aalst has a very different kind of carnival, starting with a procession of big floats. You'll need a degree in Belgian politics to work out some of the messages being delivered, but huge half-naked Vladimir Putins and bright orange Donald Trumps are instantly recognizable. You might also spot SABENA airline hostesses and Spar check-out girls - look carefully, as the vast majority of them are men wearing drag.

Photo by Andrea Kirkby on flickr:
https://www.flickr.com/photos/andreakirkb
y/6980620385/

And dragging up is a venerable Aalst tradition,
with the *voil Jeanetten* taking to the street on
Shrove Tuesday. Aalst is an industrial town
where working class men couldn't afford posh
carnival costumes, so they borrowed their
wives' cast-offs and other household items;
traditional Jeanetten wear a lampshade instead

14

of a hat, and a big (often faux) fur coat to hide whatever is or isn't underneath. Increasing numbers of women now also join the Jeannette battalions, with the same amazingly upside down fashion sense.

The Gilles of Binche throw oranges. Aalst has an onion throw instead - though most of the 'onions' are wrapped sweeties. One or two contain tickets for prizes, and in true Willie Wonka style, there's a 'golden ticket' - one lucky visitor will win a golden onion to remember Aalst for ever.

THE SINGING FESTIVALS OF ESTONIA

Prague had a Velvet Revolution. Ukraine had an Orange Revolution, Georgia had a Rose Revolution. But only the Baltic Republics had a Singing Revolution - and it was the Estonians who kicked it off.

Estonia has a tradition of choral singing that goes back to the early days of the Estonian Awakening, the nationalist movement of the nineteenth century; the first Song Festival took place in 1869, Estonian composers have a particularly strong relation with the choral tradition - works by Veljo Tormis and Arvo Part are known far outside the borders of the country. Modern Estonian Song Festivals have more than 22,000 participants, with audiences as big as 80,000 - since Estonia has a population of only 1.3 million, that's 8% of the entire country. The Song Festival is so large that it even has its own grounds - though they do host pop concerts as well.

In 1988, as cracks started to show in the USSR, Estonian protesters occupied the Song Festival grounds and started to sing patriotic Estonian songs. Eventually, they formed the Baltic Way, a human chain of 2 million people standing hand in hand between the Estonian capital Tallinn and the other two Baltic capitals.

The Song Festival is held every five years; the next one will be in 2019. The last one was the biggest ever, with 1046 choirs and 33,000 participants - will 2019 break the record again?

Lithuania and Latvia also have their song and dance festivals, both of which also go back to the 19th century. Like the Estonian Song Festival, they have become symbols of the countries' independence, and there's a strong choral singing tradition with even tiny village schools having their own choirs. Attending a Song Festival might not be top of every tourist's bucket list - but it's an unforgettable experience. Where else can you hear 30,000 people singing in beautiful harmony?

KUMBH MELA

The Kumbh Mela is the biggest of all India's religious festivals. It's also a massive logistics operation; 120 million people attended the 2013 celebration, and a huge tent city was erected, as well as numerous pontoon bridges across the river Yamuna.

It's a movable festival, too. Sometimes it takes place at the confluence of the rivers Ganga and Yamuna, at Allahabad; sometimes further up the Ganges, at Haridwar; and sometimes on other rivers - the Godavari at Nashik, or the Shipra at Ujjain. Bathing in the sacred rivers is a focal point of the festival, and cleanses a person of all their sins.

Wherever the Kumbh Mela is held, though, it's an amazing sight. All the main orders of *sadhus* (saints or hermits) in India attend; there are naked saints sitting in the ashes of their hearths, there are holy men who have held up one arm till it withered or who haven't sat down for ten years, there are yogis contorting their bodies on the sands of the river banks, and there are some hermits whose hair and beards have grown so long they can stand on them. There are encampments lit up with pictures of the gods in neon lights, and there's a fairground, too, with a Wall of Death round which daredevil motorcyclists whirl and a plaster-of-Paris Mount Meru with a real temple inside.

The climax of the Mela comes with the 'royal bath' or shahi snan ceremonies. You'll get to get up early to see the naked sadhus rush into the water before sunrise - it's crowded, it's terrifying, and it's absolutely not to be missed.

But the Mela has quieter aspects, too. Many of the *akhadas* (hermit orders) and other societies dish out meals for pilgrims, and they also hold *puja* rituals in their courtyards and tents; families take old grandfathers in their wheelchairs down to the river to bathe, and children play in the water, perhaps without really understanding what's going on around them.

Photo by Andrea Kirkby on flickr:
https://www.flickr.com/photos/andreakirkb
y/9451155791/

GERMAN BEER FESTIVALS

Everyone knows about the Oktoberfest. But Germany has a lot of beer festivals that aren't the Oktoberfest, as well as local or city festivals that strangely seem to include rather a lot of beer.

Even Munich has its alternative festival, well known to connoisseurs - the Starkbierfest, usually in March. The special strong beer was brewed for Lent; it's said that having more body in the beer qualified it as 'liquid bread' to keep pious monks going during the fast, but more likely, the alcohol simply took their minds off their hunger!

The 'strength' of the beer relates to the amount of grain used to brew it - one liter of beer amounts to almost the same as half a loaf of bread, so it *is* filling. Alcoholic strengths start at 7.5%. Unlike the Oktoberfest, this festival isn't held on the festival grounds, but actually in the breweries - but it has the same oompah bands and the same great atmosphere, plus beers that have colorful names like Salvator, Triumphator, Spekulator and Kulminator.

A new festival is the Berliner Bierfest, just 16 years old. This is the festival for anyone who loves craft beer, as it offers 2,000 world beers, many from microbreweries and innovative in style. The 'Beer mile' is just that - a whole swathe of the city given up to open air bars, a sort of urban beer garden that's just right for the first weekend in August. Fortunately, there's a 'taster' glass available as well as the traditional liter 'mass', so visitors can sample different beers without falling over after the first two or three...

Fairs like the Bremen Freimarket combine all the fun of the fair - waltzers, swing-boats and big dippers - with a lot of beer. The Freimarkt runs during the last two weeks of October. And for true single-mindedness, there's the Kulmbach Bierwoche, at the end of July. All beer, nothing else - no fairground rides, no parades, just beer.

But perhaps the nicest way to discover German festivals is just to pick any decent sized town and look for its local fair - like the Regensburg 'Buergerfest'. Each town has its own brewery - Regensburg has four - and you'll get the local brew, which you probably won't have tried before.

A FESTIVAL OF MINI-MES

The Alasitas festival in Bolivia starts towards the end of January, and like many January festivals its focus is on the new year. Bolivians don't make New Year's resolutions, though; instead, they make a wish. Or, indeed, several wishes.

Suppose you want a new house. An American approach would be to work out how much you need to save each week to have your deposit scraped together by the end of the year. But at Alasitas, you'd simply buy a model house. That's your dream. Then you take it to a shaman to get it blessed. If you're a good Catholic - many Bolivians believe in both alternatives - you might also get it sprinkled with holy water.

The markets of La Paz do a thriving trade in miniature items before Alasitas. You can get a model house, a miniature car, or wads of tiny dollar bills; you can even get a miniature degree certificate. If you fancy a spot of traveling, buy a mini-suitcase. "Honey, I shrunk the kids" has nothing on shrinking your furniture - miniature chairs, tables, sofas and even wide screen TVs are all available, if that happens to be your desire for the year.

And don't forget to do appropriate homage to the jolly little deity of the festival, Ekeko, in his poncho and beanie hat. He loves cash, but even more, he loves a drink and a smoke - so keep him supplied if you want your dreams to come true.

FIGHTING FESTIVALS

Fighting festivals are good fun, as long as you don't take them too seriously. In Thailand, the new year is celebrated with the Songkran festival, in which people throw water at each other. It might have started with just a couple of pots of water, but now many people grab water pistols and even hosepipes to ensure maximum soakage rates.

India's Holi is a festival of colors. Many people paint their faces and their clothes. But the fighting aspect of the festival is the flinging of colored powders and liquid dyes - everyone gets covered.

Spain, for some reason, seems to love a good fight as long as it involves food. In Ibi, the Els Farinats festival sees revelers spraying each other with flour. Fire extinguishers join in the fun, and there are always a few who decide to get their revenge with a tray or two of eggs. In Buñol, near Valencia, it's tomatoes that get used in a squishy, squashy celebration, and La

25

Tomatina has spawned a number of imitators with food fights in Twin Lakes, Colorado; Sutamarchan, Colombia; Dongguan, in China; and Reno, Nevada. But wickedest of all, in Haro, northern Spain, combatants fling buckets of wine at each other. White tee-shirts are soon empurpled, and the smell of the festival is amazing - and there's no rule against taking a quick swig before you throw the rest of the wine in the air.

THE ODDEST JAPANESE SHRINE FESTIVALS

Every Japanese shrine has a festival. Many are quite respectable religious festivals with a parade and a bit of incense burning, but some are, not to put to fine a point on it, completely crazy.

At Hadaka Matsuri in Nara, men are allowed to wear only loincloths (think posing pouch - these loincloths don't leave much to the imagination), and join the rugby scrum to grab the lucky charms thrown into the crowd by one of the priests. At Hitori Zumo, Omi Island, it's a single sumo wrestler who does battle - with empty air; more acting than sumo, and usually with a few laughs thrown in.

There's a sake-drinking competition at the Dorome Matsuri festival, and a competition for which baby can cry loudest at Sensoji temple, Tokyo; and an inter-school fireworks competition in Chichibu. Best of the competitions is the tug-of-war at Kasama, not so much for the tug-of-war itself as for the fact

27

that swearing isn't just encouraged, it's obligatory. (A chance to learn some of those Japanese words your teacher won't tell you.)

OSTENSION! PARDON?

Two provinces of France have remarkable religious festivals, in which the whole community often takes part.

In Limousin, the Ostensions take place every seven years (the last was in 2016). The city of Limoges starts with a torchlight procession in which the reliquary of St Martial is taken out of the cathedral and paraded around - as it has been, regularly, since the year 994. After Limoges, numerous other towns hold their own Ostension, parading the relics of their own local saint - Saint Julien de Brioude at Rochechouart, St Psalmet at Eymoutiers, St Eloi at Chaptelat, and you can probably guess the saints at the towns of Saint-Yreix, Saint-

Leonard-de-Noblat, Saint-Victurnien, Saint-Junien, Saint-Just-le-Martel.

While these are religious celebrations at heart, they're also a focus for community celebrations - concerts, parades, picnics, and feasts. And there's nothing quite like watching a long procession of white-clad pilgrims marching in step down a country lane, observed by the distinctly unimpressed Limousin cows.

In Brittany, the Pardons occur on the feast of the saint of a church or chapel. Those who attend are given an indulgence pardoning all their sins, hence the name. Some are small, focusing on a little chapel and holy well in the country; others are massive, like Sainte Anne d'Auray which is attended by over 20,000 pilgrims. Like the Ostensions, though the Pardons are religious festivals, there's often a holiday element - many villages import a funfair, and there's a bagpipe band procession at others.

KRAMPUS

Santa Claus is your friend - if you've been good. Krampus, if you haven't been good, is your worst nightmare.

In Austria, Krampus comes out on the 6th of December, St Nicholas' day, and stalks the streets. He's hairy, he has huge horns, and he carries chains which he rattles, and a bundle of birch branches for flogging bystanders. He's very, very scary.

There's only one way to pacify Krampus - give him a tot of schnapps. Perhaps that's why so many people love to dress up as Krampus!

RACING BOATS OF LUANG PRABANG

In the temple courtyards of Lao holy city Luang Prabang there's often an unexpected sight - a boat propped up on trestles. These immensely long boats are carved out of a single tree, and they're only used once a year, for the boat racing festival.

Each boat can take 50 paddlers; there are nearly 40 boats, and the racing is deadly serious. It's accompanied by music and feasting, of course, and there's a big street fair and market during the Boat Festival, but its religious reason is apparently to propitiate the naga spirits of the river.

LIVESTOCK IN THE CITY

A flock of sheep is an unexpected sight in Madrid - unless it's the end of October. Every autumn, the streets of Madrid ring to the sound of sheep bells and bleating, as shepherds drive their flocks through the city to maintain their right to the centuries-old migration route. Every spring the sheep head north to graze, and every autumn they return - passing through the center of the city - heading south to overwinter in a less chilly climate, a bit like many of the tourists who come to watch them.

BURNING MAN

In 1986, a few friends met on Baker Beach in San Francisco for a solstice bonfire party. They built, and then torched, an effigy made of driftwood, and named it 'Burning Man'. A little later, it relocated to the Black Rock Desert, and in 1997 the events became a formally administered festival.

It's still going strong, and its anarchic roots are still much in evidence; it's a festival for creators not consumers, in which many of the large scale artworks are the result of collaboration, or are designed to invite interaction. Many attendees fondly remember the Great Trojan Horse Pull, and the only way of getting a car on site is to transform it into a Mutant Vehicle (the rule is, if the car underneath can still be recognized, it's not Mutant enough). While some counterculture festivals, like Glastonbury, have gone mainstream, Burning Man has stuck to its roots, making it a great experience for the creative and open-minded.

PAGANS IN EUROPE

Jaanipaev, or St John's Day, is a huge festival in Estonia. Town centers are deserted as everyone packs beer, vodka and sausages, and heads for the woods or the beach. There will be bonfires, there will be barbecue, and there will be madness.

Celebrating Jaanipaev is a tradition that comes down from pre-Christian days. But it's also tied up - like the Song Festival - with Estonia's new nationhood, and the President now lights one of the bonfires to celebrate. Which, I reckon, makes the President of Estonia the only European head of state to take part in a pagan ritual as part of her official duties.

DAY OF THE DEAD

Halloween is for sissies. Mexico's Day of the Dead is hardcore - grinning skulls, dancing skeletons, and a colorful carnival of ghoulishly dressed dancers. Sugar candy skulls, marzipan coffins, and skeleton-papercuts decorate family altars, and even bread comes shaped like human bones for the duration. While the day celebrates the Christian All Souls' Day, the skull-obsession seems to come straight from Aztec culture. And the festivities aren't complete till you've put on your own skeleton costume for a night on the town.

By the way, the Spanish is *Dia de Muertos*. It's only Anglophones who have back-translated it from Day of the Dead to Dia de *los* Muertos.

AMAZING LANDSCAPES

HILLS THAT MAKE PERFECT CONES

The Chocolate Hills of Bohol Province in the Philippines are positively uncanny. Each hill is perfectly conical, each rising from the plain to a gently rounded top - and there are hundreds and hundreds of them. Most of the year they're covered by short grass and look pleasantly green, but in the dry season the grass dries out to a dark brown - hence the 'chocolate' name.

There are numerous legends about how these hills got to be here. Two giants threw lumps of earth at one another, and the hills are what's left of the battle; or a lovesick giant cried, and his huge teardrops fossilized, and made the hills. There's another version - a greedy giant buffalo that had eaten too much left a trail of droppings all the way through the province, and that's how the hills came to be.

In fact, the hills are a remarkable development of limestone karst geology. Limestone is always porous and prone to erosion by water; any limestone landscape will have features carved out by water - sometimes caves, sinkholes, or gorges. In 'cockpit karst', like the Chocolate Hills, the hills could have been formed by a large number of sinkholes collapsing into each other, and eventually leaving only the hills standing proud - over time, the hills have been worn smooth by wind and rain. Another explanation that's been offered is that fractures in the limestone offered an easy path for tropical rain to penetrate the stone and wear away the spaces between the hills. No one's quite sure.

However, you can be quite sure of one thing. The Chocolate Hills *aren't* made of chocolate.

Photo by P199 under CCbySA 3.0

DUNES WHERE YOU DON'T EXPECT THEM

Everyone expects sand dunes in the Sahara, or in the Empty Quarter of Arabia. But what about Norfolk, Lithuania, or the Caribbean?

If you get lost in Winterton Dunes you won't die of thirst; you'll just be a bit late at the local pub. But these dunes on the North Sea coast are the real thing, covering over 400 hectares. Some are topped by scrub or marram grass, but there are isolated spots which do feel like a real sandy desert; local wildlife includes the uncommon natterjack toad, with a yellow stripe down its back, and colonies of the little tern and dark green fritillary butterfly.

The Curonian Spit in Lithuania - a 98 kilometer long curved sliver of land separating the Baltic Sea from an inland lagoon - has sand dunes all along its length. The best known are near the village of Nida; in fact, Nida has several times been buried by shifting sand, and had to move site, most recently in the 1730s. Reforestation has claimed some of the dunes, but there are still wide expanses of sand. Best of all, winter visitors can walk on snow-topped dunes.

There are even dunes in the Caribbean; the Dominican Republic has a dune desert at Bani, stretching 15 kilometers along the ocean shore, with dunes up to 35 meters tall. Sandboarding the dunes has become quite a trend, but there's always the chance of ending up in a cactus. Ouch!

The largest dune in Europe is in France. Just off the Bay of Arcachon, the great dune of Pilat reaches 110 meters above the sea - it's just a remnant, though, of the original dunes which covered the whole area. Now, the summit gives views of the great pine forests that were planted in the nineteenth century.

However, all these dunes pale into insignificance compared to the majestic Dune 7 in Namibia, a star-shaped dune that's 383 meters tall - or the tallest of them all, Cerro Blanco in Peru's Nazca desert, which comes in at 1176 meters and takes four hours to climb - and a matter of minutes to get down by sandboard.

SALT DESERTS, SALT LAKES, SALT SEAS

There are deserts and there are deserts. Bolivia's Salar de Uyuni has no sand dunes - it's completely flat - but it's unforgettable; all white, all flat, all salt. On a good day the surrounding mountains are reflected in the salt. It's enormous, too, covering over 10,000 square kilometers. (One of its lesser known attractions is a train cemetery - railway lines were built in the 1890s, but when the mining industry collapsed, the locomotives and wagons were just abandoned here.)

The Salar is a salt desert, but there are also salt lakes. Many of these are beautifully colored, because high salinity encourages certain types of microbes which turn the water pink. Lake Hillier in Australia, Lake Koyakshoe in the Crimea, and Tanzania's Lake Natron, are all rose-colored. Better still, open-air saltings like those in Guerande, Brittany often display pools at different stages of evaporation, with colors from lurid green and gentle turquoise to dark red.

Chott el Djerid, in the Tunisian Sahara, is another salt lake, actually below sea level, which has remarkable changing colors - white, green, and purplish red. It's 250 km long, though in places it narrows to only 20 km wide; it's the largest salt pan in the entire Sahara. In the desert summers, it dries out almost entirely and can even be crossed by car - though not with complete safety, because it's just too easy to break through the salt crust to the ooze beneath.

JAIN PILGRIMAGE MOUNTAINS

Hindu holy places are often on rivers, like the Ganges, which is considered sacred. Jain holy places, on the other hand, are most often on mountains or hills, making them both picturesque and hard - in some cases extremely hard - to get to.

Sonagiri, near Gwalior, is quite a small hill, surrounded by plains where green fields mix with the red earth used for local brickmaking kilns. There are plenty of little hills like this in the region, but what makes Sonagiri special is that it's covered with little Jain temples. Inside the perimeter wall (where pilgrims leave shoes and socks at the gate), the path leads up past shrines, on steps where peacocks spread their fans, to the whitewashed temples on the peak.

Shatrunjaya, outside the little Gujarati town of Palitana, is much bigger; the mountain takes an hour or so to climb, and the temple compound is the size of a city. It's a city where only the gods are allowed to stay overnight; every sunset the great door is closed, and remains shut till sunrise the next day. From the top there are views over the plains of Saurashtra and the Gulf of Cambay, and once a year a huge pilgrimage takes Jains 18 kilometers along the ridge of the hill to another small shrine, and then down to a massive tent city for celebrations.

Photo by Andrea Kirkby:
https://www.flickr.com/photos/andreakirkby/14319623077/i

Not far from Palitana is Girnar, a hill that's sacred to both Jains and Hindus and known as the "ten thousand steps". The track climbs up through rain forest to the great Jain temples; many older pilgrims take a 'doli', a chair borne on the shoulders of porters. Above the Jain temples, a narrower track leads up even further to Hindu shrines perched on tiny peaks.

But the biggest of all is Parasnath, in Jharkand, eastern India. This mountain is so big it's clearly visible from the Allahabad-Calcutta railway line. It has its own pilgrimage village at the base, full of dharamsalas where pilgrims can spend the night. Most get up in the early hours to tackle the mountain, visiting several shrines on a circuit before finishing at the temple on the highest peak. Some still go barefoot - though that's not required - on this 1,365 meter high mountain.

CROOKED TREES AND CROOKED FORESTS

Trees are funny things. Sometimes they grow straight, and sometimes they grow crooked. And sometimes, no one knows exactly why, an entire forest decides to grow crooked.

In Gryfino, north-west Poland, there's a grove of 400 pines, all of which have the same bend in their trunks, making them look like a forest of upside-down question marks. It's almost certain that they were trained to grow that way - but why? No one knows.

There's another bunch of pines that wiggle and squiggle, this time in free form, on the Curonian Spit by the Baltic Sea, at Kruglaya, Kaliningrad. The reason for these contortions might be a caterpillar that eats young shoots - deprived of their lead shoot, these trees ended up growing sideways - though some have have also suggested strong winds, human manipulation, and even supernatural forces.

There's a twisted forest in Utah, too - a grove of prehistoric bristlecone pines that have become gnarled and contorted with age. As portions of the bristlecone die out, the rest of the tree grows on, resulting in tortured twists and turns. No one's saying quite how old these bristlecones are, but the oldest, named Methuselah, is 4,675 years old and grows in eastern California; these ones are younger, but not by a lot.

Aokigahara forest, in the shadow of Mount Fuji, is twisted for another reason; it's become a place that many people head to die - the 'suicide forest'. But it's also an amazing natural sight - its earlier nickname was 'the sea of trees' - where thick forest has grown up over a hard lava floor. The trees are so thick that the wind can't be felt inside the forest, and their roots twist and contort as they try to find a way through the rock. Which doesn't make it sound all that attractive - but in fact the marked trails are popular with hikers.

LITTLE VOLCANOES INSIDE BIGGER

VOLCANOES

Volcanoes always represent a geological work in progress. In many cases, old volcanoes have - quite literally - blown their tops, creating a huge caldera, only for smaller volcanoes to start growing up in the middle.

Mount Bromo, in Indonesia, is only part of the much large Tengger caldera, a collapsed volcano that measures 10 kilometres across and includes the famous 'sea of sand'. While most tourists head for a sunrise view of Bromo from the rim, and then climb Bromo itself, it's possible to walk round the rim of the caldera to take advantage of the extensive views.

At Santorini in Greece the twin islands of Santorini and Thirassia represent what's left of the caldera formed by an eruption several hundred thousand years ago - the sea has eroded much of the rest. In the middle, the little island of Nea Kameni has started growing

47

back up again - it's now 130 meters high, and visitors can sniff the bad egg smell of its sulfur vents, or swim in waters warmed by geothermal activity.

Dallol volcano, in Ethiopia, is a bit different. Here, a volcano sits in the middle of thick salt deposits. It's never managed to struggle up to more than 48 meters in height, but it's spectacular all the same thanks to the vibrant colors created by the mix of sulfur and salt. Bright pink and red clash with lurid green and yellow, and the salt crystals form strange shapes like overgrown tree roots or lichen.

THE ONLY MALE RIVER IN INDIA

All Indian rivers are female: Ganga, Jumna, Godavari, Cauvery, and the invisible Saraswati. Only the Brahmaputra is male.

Starting in Tibet as the Tsangpo, the Brahmaputra enters India in the north-eastern state of Arunachal Pradesh, and runs through Assam to the border with Bangladesh, where it meets the Ganges and loses itself in the maze of the Ganges delta. It carves a massive swathe through Assam, dividing into a number of different, braided channels; in places, it's 20 kilometers wide, and at its narrowest point (the state capital, Guwahati) it's still over 1 km in width.

It also claims to possess one of the world's biggest river islands, Majuli, some 352 square kilometers in extent. With 22 Vaishnavite monasteries surviving from an original 65 foundations, it's also a holy island with a unique culture, including drumming and masked dances.

SVANETI, TUSHETI, KHEVSURETI - LANDS

THAT TIME FORGOT

Tucked away in the Caucasian mountains of Georgia are three tiny enclaves, Svaneti, Tusheti, and Khevsureti, with their own cultures and ancient traditions. Tusheti and Khevsureti aren't even accessible for the whole year - the dangerous roads are impassable in winter - and in many cases, villages are abandoned in the autumn, leaving only a single caretaker behind.

These have always been rough places to live; the defensive towers which line the valleys are one of the most characteristic sights of the region. Ushguli, one of the world's highest continually occupied villages at 2,100 meters, has a huge concentration of tower houses and retains a single tower from the medieval palace of Queen Tamara. Fortunately the towers are no longer used as fortresses; some have been adapted as guest-houses for the increasing number of tourists. But while the locals are, by and large, peaceable, there are still wolves in some areas, and the fierce Caucasian sheepdog remains a threat to hikers.

WADI NAKHR - THE UNKNOWN GRAND CANYON

Oman is a funny country. You'd expect somewhere in Arabia to have sand dunes (and it does, the wonderful Wahiba Sands), but a 3,000 meter mountain? And a kilometer-deep grand canyon?

Jebal Shams, 'Sun Mountain', is quite a popular attraction, though only the south summit is accessible to hikers (the north summit has a military base on it). However, it's Wadi Nakhr, which runs up to the flank of the mountain, which offers the most fascinating experience. Dropping down from the plateau, a narrow path enters the gorge and runs along the side, as a balcony walk between the sheer cliff above and precipice below, to a ruined village above a massive rock arch. A shallow cave under the canyon end shelters a pool of clear water, a refreshing end to one of the Middle East's scariest hikes.

BAMBOO FORESTS

Sagano Bamboo Forest, near Kyoto, is not just a wonderful sight; it's a wonderful sound, included by the Ministry of the Environment on its 'top 100 Soundscapes of Japan'. It's not by any means the only bamboo forest in Japan, or even in Kyoto, but it's the classic - the best known bamboo forest in the world.

But other places have them too. La Bambouseraie, near Nimes in southern France, was begun in 1856 as a botanical garden; when a frost killed most of the other plants in the 1950s, the owners decided to concentrate on the survivors - the bamboos - and the garden is now a huge bamboo forest with shady alleys and even a Zen garden.

The Rutgers Gardens bamboo forest in New Jersey is another attractive bamboo grove full of the aggressive bamboo *phyllostachys nigra*. As anyone who has planted this vandal bamboo in their back garden will know, it grows like nobody's business and it's next to impossible to get rid of. Fortunately, the Rutgers Gardens have over 60 acres of space, so the bamboo's plans for world domination aren't such a problem.

JOKULHLAUPS AND JOKULSARLON

Iceland has some marvelously unpronounceable attractions. Once you know that 'jokul' means a glacier, things get a bit easier.

A jokulhlaup is what happens when glacial melt water breaks out from behind an ice dam

- for instance when a volcano has started melting the ice. Iceland has simmered down a bit in recent centuries, but jokulhlaups have created immense river canyons. The Jokulsarglufur gorge in the extreme north of the country was formed by a flood with four and half times more water flow than the Amazon river, and it's undeniably impressive, with several huge waterfalls along its length.

Not to be confused with the very different Jokulsarlon, a huge glacial lagoon on the east coast. The Breithamerkurjokull glacier calves huge icebergs into the lagoon, where they slowly float towards the narrow exit channel.

Things change rapidly in Iceland. Surtsey island didn't exist in 1962. By the end of 1967, it had a name. But as wind and wave eat away at the little volcanic rock, geologists estimate that the island could disappear again by the end of this century.

LIKE A PAINTING

Chinese paintings always look like something out of a dream. Hills that go straight up, like mushrooms, in mist and clouds - that can't be real, surely?

At Zhangjiajie, it is. Rock pillars soar from narrow bases all the way to their tree-covered tops, hundreds of meters without a break. The whole Wulingyuan scenic district features sandstone pillars and deep ravines, with deep green vegetation setting off the brown and gray of the landscape. It couldn't be more like a painting.

The karst landscapes of the Guilin Li river also look unbelievably painterly. The hills start right from the horizontal flood plain and mushroom upwards, row on row of little conical hills interspersed with massive blockish peaks. Some mountains even seem to lean over backwards. They dwarf the little cruise boats that ply the river below.

Best of all, perhaps, is Huangshan National Park, where seas of clouds gather between the jagged peaks. Here, pine trees crown the ridges, while below there are gorges to hike and shallow rushing rivers. Some of the ancient pine look almost as if they've been trained to contort themselves into weird shapes - you'd suspect them of being bonsai trees if they weren't life size.

For those who can't visit the Chinese national parks, there's an alternative to paintings. Scholars collected rocks known as gongshi which had all the qualities of a beautiful landscape, and put them on rosewood pedestals. A good gongshi is a miniature mountain, and those who appreciate them say you can get the same aesthetic experience from spending time with a gongshi that you can floating down the Guilin Li on a boat.

GORGES OF SOUTHERN FRANCE

Southern France has nothing quite like the Grand Canyon, but it does have two gorges with quite amazing characters.

The Gorges de la Frau, in the Ariege department, are a series of gorges 300 to 400 meters deep and more than three kilometers long, gouged out by the river Hers. 'Frau' is from the same root as the word 'fracture', and this gorge marks a decisive break, with white cliffs soaring up on both sides. The gorge has got its own microclimate, markedly wetter and cooler than the surrounding area.

The Verdon Gorge, in Provence, is much bigger - 25 kilometers long and up to 700 meters deep where the Verdon river cuts its way through limestone rocks. Its beauty is accentuated by the bright turquoise color of the river, which comes from minerals scoured out by glaciers and washed down in the water.

Then there's the Ardeche - 25 kilometers of meandering, swooping river, with beautiful green woods at the bottom of a wide gorge flanked by high limestone cliffs. There are caves, too, and even a limestone arch that soars over the river at one point.

But not everyone loves the gorges. One local dismissed the Verdon gorge as "agriculturally useless." Which, given its wild beauty, is probably a good thing.

HIGH CUP NICK

Lots of people know that the Pennine Way starts with Kinder Scout. They've heard of the Tan Hill Pub, too. But the biggest landscape attraction of the famous hiking route is almost unsung (though often photographed); High Cup Nick.

It's a nick - almost as if someone took a penknife and carved a slot in the side of the hill. It's reached by a long slog in almost featureless moorland, which gives no sign of developing into anything more than another ten miles of moorland. Then suddenly, the ground drops away, and there are views all the way over the plains as far as the glimmering line of gray that marks the coast.

THE NOT QUITE EMPTY QUARTER

The Empty Quarter isn't actually empty; it's full of sand, if nothing else. This corner of the Arabian peninsula is 250,000 square miles of desert; sand dunes, and just occasionally, salt flats. The climate is hyper-arid, though a few small plants manage to survive, as do small rodents and spiders.

It has exercised a strong appeal for explorers over the decades. Wilfred Thesiger crossed the sands several times with Bedouin tribes he knew; more recently, Alastair Humphreys and Leon McCarron walked from Salalah, in Oman, to Dubai, after their funding for a South Pole expedition fell through, and a South Korean team made a similar trip in 2013. As Shelley wrote (though about somewhere completely different), "the long and level sands stretch far away" - and that emptiness is what attracts.

Fortunately for locals, the Empty Quarter is full of one other thing besides sand: oil.

MACABRE SIGHTS

CREMATION WATCHING

You wouldn't have thought that watching dead bodies being burned would be so compulsive, but in several places around the globe it's become a major tourist sight.

Varanasi, India, is one of the holy places of Hinduism, situated on the sacred Ganges river. That's why many Hindus choose to be cremated here, on the banks of the Ganges; after the cremation, their ashes are scattered over the river waters.

A slightly different ritual is observed by many tourists, who come to hang over the railings at Manikarnika Ghat and watch the cremations, often several dozen going on simultaneously. Above the ghat, huge piles of wood - expensive in a greatly deforested country - stand for selection by the deceased's relatives. Other tourists sit in the Blue Lassi cafe and watch the funeral parties carrying shrouded bodies on their shoulders down the road outside.

In Bali, Indonesia, cremations are expensive rituals; often, bodies are temporarily buried while a family, or even a whole village, saves up for the occasion. The procession, including a massive model bull and a tall bamboo tower, makes its way from the deceased's house to the burning ground, accompanied by gamelan orchestras, dancers, and offerings. It's an amazing spectacle. Then the tower and the bull - containing the coffin - are set on fire. Tourists often follow the procession - on one occasion actually getting up on the pyre to take pictures inside the coffin!

Photo by Andrea Kirkby on flickr:
https://www.flickr.com/photos/andreakirkb
y/24715359821

If seeing other people get burned isn't enough,
tourists can experience cremation for
themselves at a theme park in Shanghai - or at
least, a simulation, in which they're put in a
coffin and sent through a blast of hot air as the
climax of a gruesome funeral ride. That's a bit
like the 'death schools' in Korea where

'students' practice lying in a coffin and think about their lives. (That may not be completely unconnected to the high suicide rate in the country.)

But weirder than all this is the German phenomenon of 'corpse tourism'. Germany's burial and cremation regulations are highly restrictive, making funerals extremely expensive. Cremains have to be buried in a full-size plot or put in a columbarium - you can't just scatter the ashes (though if you live in Bremen, you *can* bury them in your garden). So some dead bodies take a holiday and go off traveling - to the Netherlands, the Czech Republic, or Switzerland, where the rules aren't as strict and costs are much lower.

BOOKS BOUND IN HUMAN SKIN

The Moyses Hall museum in Bury St Edmunds, England, contains a fascinating exhibit related to William Corder, who was hanged in 1828 after murdering his lover Maria Marten. There's a death mask. There are details of the murder. And there's a nice leather bound book - which when you look closely at the label turns out to be a book bound in Corder's flayed skin. In a nice piece of poetic justice, it turns out to be an account of his trial.

A distant relative of Corder recently asked for various relics (which include his scalp and ear) to be returned for burial - but was turned down by the museum.

Corder wasn't the only one; Bristol's M Shed museum contains an account of the trial of John Horwood, who beat a girl to death with a rock - and that too bound is bound in the executed criminal's skin. The Royal College of Surgeons in Edinburgh has a notebook bound in the skin of William Burke, the 'resurrection man' who supplied Edinburgh doctors with corpses for dissection, and started his career as a murderer when he couldn't get enough fresh corpses out of the cemetery.

There's even a word - or two - for this phenomenon: anthropodermic bibliopegy. Fortunately, it seems to have been a rather short-lived fashion.

THE MOST SKULLS IN THE WORLD, EVER

The Celtic acropolis of Roquepertuse, near Marseilles in France, was discovered in the nineteenth century and was immediately celebrated as evidence of the Celtic skull cult. Each of the great pillars that supported the front of the temple had head-shaped niches cut into it, many of which were filled with skulls. Gruesome - but with only a dozen skulls all told.

The basilica of Otranto holds many more. The Romanesque church is most well known for its stunning mosaic pavement, which shows the tree of life, stories from medieval romances, mermaids, seahorses and tigers; but in a side chapel, three huge glass fronted cupboards behind the altar hold the skulls of the martyrs of Otranto. A Turkish force invaded Otranto in 1480 and massacred the town's 813 defenders, allegedly because they wouldn't convert to Islam (though possibly just because their families couldn't pay a big enough ransom). That beats Roquepertuse by quite a few hundred skulls.

But another Ottoman atrocity, the Tower of Skulls in Nis, Serbia, edges Otranto out of the running. This stone tower was built in 1809 with niches to contain the skulls of Serbian rebels against the Ottoman empire, after they blew up a powder magazine, killing themselves and quite a few Ottoman soldiers. Now housed inside a little chapel, this tower contains 952 skulls.

At St Leonard's church in Hythe, England, there are reputed to be 2,000 skulls in the ossuary under the church. This isn't down to a massacre - the graveyard simply ran out of space, and so old bodies were dug up to make room for new. They're neat and tidy and in their way, rather charming.

But two other sites beat St Leonard's hands down. In Phnom Penh, Cambodia, the memorial stupa at Choeung Ek contains 5,000 skulls of victims of the Pol Pot regime. Evora, Portugal, has a chapel entirely decorated with human bones under the Franciscan church, made to remind visitors of their own mortality - and this, too, has about 5,000 skulls.

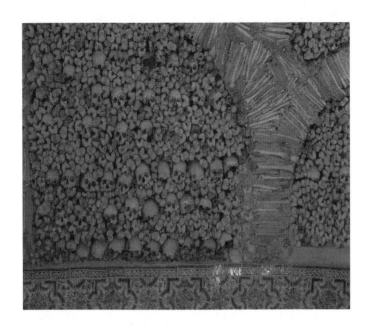

Photo by Andrea Kirkby on flickr:
https://www.flickr.com/photos/andreakirkby/24599251982/

But the winner of the most skulls in the world competition is the ruins of Tenochtitlan, Mexico. Archaeologists recently discovered the Huey tzompantli, or tower of skulls. The Aztecs were, to put it gently, not too observant of the Geneva Convention, being given to sacrifices in which they ripped out victims' hearts and then sliced off their heads for decorating the skull-racks. Archaeologists have already found 136,000 skulls in Tenochtitlan (though admittedly only 650 in this particular tower), and there may be more to come.

DEATH COMES FOR THE EMPEROR

The Kapuzinergruft in Vienna has been the burial place of Habsburg emperors since 1633; 12 emperors, 18 empresses, and 145 royalty altogether have made their eternal home here, the latest being Otto von Habsburg, the man who refused the crown of Spain (Juan Carlos accepted it from Franco instead).

The original crypt has been expanded numerous times; Maria Theresa extended it past the church and under the monastery garden, building a dome that admits natural light into part of the mausoleum. There's still space for a few more tombs, even though there are no more emperors.

Stars of the show are the great sarcophagi, some decorated with crowned skulls and heraldic designs, others just simple coffin-shaped boxes with a single skull and crossbones or a crown modeled on top. Maria Theresa's splendid monument is a great Baroque confection with military trophies, angels, allegorical figures, and at the top the figures of Maria Theresa herself with her husband Franz Stephen gazing into each others' eyes.

You can't take it with you, they say. But the Habsburg emperors at least managed to make a very stylish exit.

THE DOUBLE DECKER AND THE DANCE OF

DEATH

The fifteenth and sixteenth centuries were a rather morbid period. Recurrent plagues and high infant mortality didn't help, but there was a definite darkening of outlook as the middle ages came to their end, and this is reflected in a number of monuments.

The "double decker" cadaver tomb shows the deceased on top, as they would have been in life, often in robes of state; but underneath, they're shown as a corpse, with a disheveled shroud, ribs open to view, and worms crawling in and out. The message is a stark one - "We all come to this," or in the words of Thomas Gooding, whose wall slab in Norwich cathedral features a friendly skeleton bust, "As you are now even so was I, And as I am so shall you be." These tombs are found all over Europe, including one in St Peter's Basilica and fine clerics' tombs in Winchester, Canterbury, and Lincoln cathedrals.

The Dance of Death also belongs to this strain of morbid sentiment, and paintings of the Dance often decorated cemetery walls. It penetrated Europe from the extreme north all the way to the furthest south - there's a wonderful version in Tallinn, Estonia, as well as two Istrian churches, Hrastovlje in Slovenia and Skriljinah in Croatia. The most famous version nowadays, though, is the series of woodcuts created by Hans Holbein.

FROM THE HOUSE OF THE DEAD

Sometimes the dead are better housed than the living. Some of the glorious Victorian mausoleums of London's cemeteries, for instance, are actually bigger than the average new apartment.

Bratislav Stojanovic, a homeless Serbian, noticed this, and decided after some while living in abandoned houses to make his home in Nis city cemetery. It had the advantage that the open tomb he found was well insulated, being underground, and the police didn't bother him there.

In Manila, thousands of Filipinos have set up home in the North Cemetery. The population of about 6,000 even have their own school and a 'jeepney' transit system. Some inhabitants work as gravediggers or coffin makers, while others hawk goods on the streets outside for a living. Only one mod con is lacking - there's no electricity.

In Cairo, Egypt, the City of the Dead has been home to poor families for centuries. The ancient Egyptians, famously, had an interesting relationship with death, building immense temples and pyramids, and mummifying their bodies to preserve them for ever; but this city is an Islamic graveyard, and the families that live in the tombs are simply people who can't afford anywhere else.

THE DEAD CENTRE OF NEW ORLEANS

New Orleans is where Southern Gothic meets voodoo, and the Vampire Lestat meets the zombie. So it's hardly surprising that New Orleans cemeteries are a big tourist draw, with many companies providing tours of the cemeteries.

These cemeteries are unusual, because no one's buried below ground. The water table in New Orleans is so high in this below-sea-level city that digging a hole doesn't make any sense, so coffins are put in high gabled mausolea where the swamp can't get at them.

Not all the residents are real - or dead. Movie star Nicolas Cage has built himself a pyramid in St Louis no 1 cemetery, though when we last checked he was still alive and kicking, and Lafayette Cemetery is most famed for its fictional resident Lestat and the equally fictional Mayfair Witches.

INDUSTRIAL AND POST-

INDUSTRIAL

Industrial and post-industrial tourism has become popular, particularly with urban explorers. Thirty years ago, someone visiting old lime kilns and factories was either an industrial archeology nerd or a photographer looking for moody shots - now, industrial tourism has gone mainstream.

FORDLANDIA AND THE RUINS OF DETROIT

Brazil's Fordlandia was started by Henry Ford as a prefab town to supply his US car plants with rubber. It was a daring project, but it failed; begun in 1928, by 1934 workforce riots and mismanagement had destroyed its raison d'etre, and when the manager absconded, it was time to give up.

Most of the original buildings still stand, including the iconic water tower. Oddly, Fordlandia has had something of a revival recently, as people looking for cheap housing have taken over some of the old buildings; there are now a couple of thousand people living there, more than at any time since the 1930s.

Henry Ford realized Fordlandia wasn't working, but he would have been surprised to see Detroit as an industrial ruin. In fact, nowadays Detroit gets more visitors interested in taking photos of its ruined factories, train station, mansions and churches than it does any other kind of business. Michigan Central Station, in particular, makes an impressive statement in its semi-ruined state - though 2015 saw some renovation work on the structure.

Perhaps it's the contrast between the wealth of Detroit's golden age shown in its luxurious and ambitious buildings, and their current ruined state, that makes the city such an attraction for 'ruin porn'. It's our version of the medieval *memento mori* - a reminder that all things are prone to change and decay.

THE BIG COPPER MOUNTAIN

Stora Kopparberg ('big copper mountain' in Swedish) was given a charter by King Magnus in 1347 - though the bishop of Vasteras' share certificate is even earlier, dating from 1288. It was probably the first limited liability company ever created, and at its height, mined two-thirds the world's entire production of copper in its great mine in the town of Falun.

Things changed. Huge copper mines in the Americas made the relatively small scale of production in Sweden uneconomic, and the Stora Kopparberg company invested in other activities (pulp, paper and forestry); in 1992 the mine closed down for good.

The great Falun mine is now a museum. There are displays telling the story of the mine and the town, as well as retailing myths and legends from the old days. But the real attraction for many tourists is the damp, cold and dark trip into the depths of the mine and its narrow, criss-crossing passages.

THE WHITE PYRAMIDS

Egypt has its pyramids - and so does Cornwall. There's even a pub in St Austell called "The White Pyramid".

These aren't tombs or monuments to past monarchs. They're a testament to the geology of the area and the china clay industry which dominated this part of Cornwall for nearly 200 years. Now, most of deposits here have been abandoned, though there's still a good half-century's worth of kaolin in them, but the white pyramids remain. Grass has now covered some of them, and they have a new name - the Cornish Alps.

There's a China Clay Country Park, and the Wheal Martyn Heritage Museum tells the story of the industry; and Charlestown, which handled a great deal of the early trade, is now a beautifully archaic early Georgian port which sees more film crews than it does china clay cargoes. In many places, fading industry has left wastelands behind; but here, it seems to have left only beauty behind.

TAKE IT WITH A PINCH OF SALT

Wieliczka Salt Mine is one of the big tourist attractions of southern Poland. It's an ancient mine, which opened in the 13th century as a royal monopoly, and kept producing till 1996.

However, although it's a fascinating piece of real industrial history, the main attraction is the crazily intricate work of individual miners who created chapels, statues, and monuments out of the salt. The centerpiece is a full sized church which even has chandeliers made out of salt.

There seems to be something about salt mines that brings out the crazy architect in people. At Zipaquira in Colombia, salt miners had already built a little chapel inside the mine; but in the 1950s a much bigger project started, a huge salt cathedral. In 1992, this was replaced by an even bigger cathedral - though since there's no bishop we should probably put the word 'cathedral' in quotation marks.

The salt works of Salins-les-Bains and Arc-et-Senans in eastern France are quite different. Here, there are no cathedrals - this is the work of the Enlightenment, with neo-classical architecture and an elegant semi-circular layout. Here, salt wasn't mined as a solid; instead, brine was pumped into great basins and the water slowly evaporated away. 21 kilometers of pipework connected the two production sites, which kept producing till 1962; they're now a historical monument.

HOME OF A REVOLUTION

Ironbridge Gorge was the home of the industrial revolution in England. It had several natural advantages - easily accessible deposits of coal, iron ore and limestone, and easy river access to the sea and major ports.

Here the first major cast iron bridge in the world was built in 1779, crossing the gorge of the river Severn, and now there are ten different museums and 35 historic sites within the Ironbridge area. Coalport china was made here, and the bottle kilns can still be seen; the Old Furnace, where iron was made with coke instead of charcoal for the first time in 1709, can still be seen, and there's even an entire museum devoted to the making of clay tobacco pipes.

Later industrial sites in Britain have impressively massive mills and huge furnaces. But Ironbridge shows the moment at which many trades were just leaving artisan production behind - still small in scale, but introducing the first techniques which would lead, eventually, to mass production.

CHERNOBYL AND OTHER NUCLEAR TOURS

Chernobyl No 4 Reactor at Pripyat, Ukraine, blew up on 25 April, 1986. It killed 31 people within days; no one knows how many people died as an eventual consequence of health issues brought about by radioactive contamination - quite possibly several thousand.

Now, Chernobyl tours are a popular option for travelers visiting Kyiv. It's a chance to visit a ghost town, as well as to see the remaining nuclear reactors and the concrete sarcophagus that covers the ruins of No 4.

But there are plenty of places you can visit nuclear reactors. The world's first, Experimental Breeder Reactor No 1 in Idaho, even lets visitors touch the controls, though they're not connected to anything these days, and visitors can also test their skills at manipulating the mechanical arm that workers used to move dangerous materials behind a thick protective glass wall.

Switzerland has four nuclear reactors that offer guided tours from time to time, at Muehleberg, Beznau, Goesgen and Leibstadt, as well as ZWILAG, the nuclear waste disposal center. In the UK, there are visitor centers at several power plants including Hinkley Point, Sizewell B, and Torness, and in France, several 'centrales' offer tours. Fortunately, none of them offer the Chernobyl-like experience of visiting a ghost town en route.

SLOSS FURNACES

Sloss Furnaces was a landmark of Birmingham, Alabama for years. Opened in 1882, the blast furnace produced iron for the next 90 years, finally closing in 1971.

Now, its water tower still stands proud, and the whole site has become a National Historic Landmark - one of the first industrial sites to be saved for public use. It's home to metal arts classes, concerts and shows, and also holds a Halloween event - Sloss Fright Furnace. A visitor center presents the history and gives some context to the giant structures; but it's probably the huge rusted metal buildings and the remains of the machinery that are the real attraction.

RIO TINTO AND ALMADEN MINES

Miners have been working around the Rio Tinto in southern Spain since the Romans and even before; they've dug pits, then shafts, and strip mined, and they've built towns and transport depots, railways and even English style churches.

Changing times made many of the mines obsolete by the 1990s, and they've now become tourist attractions. Rio Tinto Mining Park lets visitors enter a mining gallery, or take a ride in one of the original wooden carriages along the banks of the red river, whose waters clearly show the rusty colors of iron ore. The huge open cast mine pits make a dramatic, if sombre landscape.

Another mining park at Almaden, further north, shows a different kind of mining - mercury, derived from the bright red mineral cinnabar. Mining here stopped in 2000, and the mining park allows visitors to go down 50 meters in the old mines; most of the tour guides are former miners - a great way of providing employment for those who lost their jobs when the mine closed.

Almaden is not to be confused with New Almaden, in California. But why was the place called New Almaden? Because it, too, produced mercury, and has its own mining museum, while the old mine area has become the Quicksilver Country Park.

DEEP SEA WHALING

Not quite abandoned, the whaling station at the appropriately named Hvalfjordur ('Whale fjord'), Iceland, is a picture of desolation; brutal concrete buildings and a deserted concrete dock. Only the occasional puff of smoke from a chimney suggests it might still be in use; it's Iceland's last operational facility.

At Sudureyri, the old whaling station was deserted back in 1939. It used to employ 110 people; now no one lives there at all, though it's become an obligatory visit for photographers. Huge, rusting metal boilers and a stone chimney are all that's left of the busy whaling station.

Demand for whale meat is decreasing in Iceland, and though the country reserves the right to hunt for both minke and fin whales, it probably makes more money out of whale watching tours from Reykjavik harbor, popular with tourists who then - the hypocrites! - go off to a restaurant to try their first taste of whale meat.

WATER, WATER

EVERYWHERE

STEPWELLS AND TANKS

India has beautiful forts and temples, but it also has a form of architecture that's completely unique - the stepwell. Originally just a simple trench dug into the rock to reach water, the stepwell developed into a highly ornate and complex construction which also played an important part in the social life of many cities.

The fort at Junagadh has one of the oldest stepwells, Adi Kadi Vav, a massive ramp that runs down a great carved slot in the rock to the water. Some neighborhood stepwells in small towns still adopt this type of construction, but it wasn't good enough for kings and rajas.

At Pathan, in Gujarat, the Rani ki Vav dating from the eleventh century is perhaps the most famous of all the wells. It's 27 meters deep, with pillared pavilions and bridges over the great steps that run down towards the well. Every surface is carved with intricate sculptures showing stories of the god Vishnu and delicate nymphs, or curling foliage, and even when the sun is burning hot at the top, it's cool at the bottom of the steps by the deep well.

In the palace at Mandu, Madhya Pradesh, the designers of the royal palace added extra refinement; they linked a stepwell into the air conduits of the building so that it works as a kind of natural air-conditioning.

One of the great delights of these stepwells is their geometrical precision. In the Rajasthan village of Abhaneri, Chand Baori is almost an inverted pyramid, the sides sloping down to the green water at the bottom; its sides are criss-crossed by zigzagging steps, making an intricate but completely logical pattern. In the desert heat, the water at the bottom is six degrees cooler than on the surface, stopping it evaporating in the hot sun.

Another geometrical beauty is a little circular stepwell in Chanderi, Madhya Pradesh. Here, three separate stairways start at equally spaced

points around the circumference and curl
down the sides of the shaft, making a mandala-
like design. It's just a little neighborhood well -
unlike Chand Baori which was designed for a
king - but it still has real charm.

In Southern India, with its wetter monsoon
climate, stepwells aren't common, but instead
many temples and towns have beautiful tanks
cut in the rock to collect and hold rainwater.
There's even one whose steps form a swastika
(a Hindu lucky symbol long before the Nazis
got hold of it) near the Pundarikaksha temple
in Thiruvellarai; it's visible on Google maps.
Some tanks are just large ponds, while others
are as beautifully built as stepwells - some, like
those at Hampi, Karnataka, even have little
pavilions in the middle, presumably for
chilling out (literally) when the weather got too
hot. And the city of Bangalore was built
around a series of lakes that provided both
water and a reduced temperature for the city -
though they're now in trouble thanks to bad
pollution and poor maintenance.

Perhaps modern India should look back at some of these engineering marvels and start rethinking its water supply strategies.

MAKING WATER MOVE UPHILL

There's a big problem with rivers and canals. They're a great way to get around, until a hill gets in the way - and then you have the difficulty that water won't flow uphill.

Of course there are ways to get around that. A simple lock, with water held between two sets of lock gates, can allow a boat to navigate safely from one level to another. Even quite a big hill can be navigated by the simple expedient of making a big series of locks, like the 10 Foxton Locks or 29 Caen Hill Locks on the English canal system.

This method's not perfect though. Not only does navigating through locks take a long time, but it also wastes water - most locks need a sizable reserve pound. So engineers have been challenged to find new ways to move boats uphill, and some of their creations are quite spectacular.

The Elblag Canal in Poland uses inclined planes - ramps with rail tracks on which little carriages run. The carriages pick up the boats at the bottom and run them up to the top. There's something endearingly basic about this system. A much later (1969) and bigger version of this system, at Saint-Louis-Arzviller on the French Rhine-Marne canal, replaced a flight of 17 locks and is much more industrial in style - boats enter a huge water tank through a lock, and are carried up to the top canal in just four minutes.

Boat lifts are even more spectacular. At Strepy-Theiu in Belgium, a boat lift built in 2002 looks like a skyscraper among the green fields and hills. It lifts boats vertically for 73 meters, taking 7 minutes - but it's still smaller than the Three Gorges Dam Ship Lift in China, completed as recently as 2016 and taking just 8 minutes to lift boats of up to 3,000 tons 113 meters.

Weirdest of the lot, though, is the Falkirk Wheel, which connects the Forth & Clyde with the Union Canal in Scotland. This boat lift doesn't go straight up and down - it rotates, taking ten minutes to bring the top boat down, and the bottom boat up. It's positively boat ballet!

A MAZE OF WATERS

Irrigation systems are key to agriculture in a dry country so it's hardly a surprise that the Persians invented a great irrigation system. What's perhaps a little more surprising is that it spread all over the middle east and Europe, and even as far as the Silk Road provinces of China, and North Africa.

Persia is full of mountains, but not water; the *qanat* is a way of getting at the aquifers hidden under the mountains, and bringing water from them to the plains where it's needed. Vertical shafts like wells are dug, with the first one reaching below the water table to make a water source, but they're then connected by a gently sloping passageway which runs through the mountain and out into the irrigated land. Often, qanats contour the sides of canyons, and have complicated sluices allowing different owners to share the water supply out equally.

In Oman, the *falaj* system irrigates desert oases such as Nizwa, the former capital; the falaj is considered a prime national symbol and five of the preserved sections of old aflaj (the Arabic plural of falaj) are now recognized as UNESCO world heritage sites.

The Romans, of course, were great engineers, and when they saw the qanat they decided to pinch the idea. While the qanats of Palermo, Sicily, date from the Arab period, it was the Romans who installed a qanat in Luxembourg (the 'Raschpetzer'). The Spanish got their qanats (canals in Spanish) from the Arabs, and there are still working systems in Segovia and Seville. It was the conquistadores who took the idea with them to Peru and Chile, where the water systems are called *puquios*.

THE ICE STUPAS OF LADAKH

Ladakh is a high altitude desert, in which most villages depend for their water on glacial melt. That in turn depends on the winter storms depositing enough snow on the Himalayas; but global warming has led to a decline in the amount of snow that's falling. Worse still, the ice in the high mountains doesn't start melting till June, so the peak water flow comes long after the water's needed for planting and watering the crops.

But Ladakhis are resourceful. A solution has been found, and is now being tried out at Phyang monastery - the ice stupa.

There are thousands of sacred stupas in Ladakh, all built of stone, and most containing a small relic or a Buddhist text. Now Phyang monastery is building ice stupas, collecting the water at the end of the year when water is plentiful, building up the ice into a huge cone, and allowing it to melt over the next summer to provide water for agriculture and other purposes. Because a cone minimizes the surface area of the ice that's exposed to the sun, it keeps solid five times longer than an ice-field on the mountain slopes.

Phyang is now hoping to change the arid valley that surrounds the monastery by planting hundreds of poplar and willow trees, that will not only green the valley, but also provide income for the monastery when they're old enough to provide wood for construction.

GREAT DRAIN JOURNEYS

One of the lesser known sights of Rome is the outlet of the Cloaca Maxima. This huge drain was built to reclaim the marshy, low-lying area between the seven hills of Rome, and the massive arch through which it joins the Tiber can still be seen, just beside the Ponte Rotto.

London also has a magnificent drain, which features in fiction - notably China Mieville's *King Rat* - though it's not easily visited or seen. Joseph Bazalgette was the man who developed a new, scientific, progressive sewerage system for London in the 1860s, after the Great Stink (wonderful name!) had alerted Parliament to the problems of public sanitation, mainly because the House of Commons got the vile odors drifting through the windows.

Although the sewer itself isn't visible, its course is easy to follow; the main interceptor is incorporated in the Thames Embankment, underneath the road. Meanwhile, the Crossness Pumping station - an extravaganza of gleaming brass and spectacular decorative ironwork - runs regular open days, giving a good feel for the grandeur of Bazalgette's grand design.

In Paris, tourists can visit the sewers, which have been offering tours since 1867. The modern system was put in place by Baron Haussmann, and reflects in its size and grandiosity the same ideals which Haussmann employed in creating his wide, straight boulevards. Paris below ground reflects Paris above.

New York doesn't run a sewer tour, but it runs visits to Newton Creek wastewater plant. With acerbic New Yorker humor, they decided to open the plant on Valentine's Day.

CANAL CITIES

It can get a bit wearying to be told that St Petersburg is "the Venice of the North", or Udaipur "the Venice of the East". So we won't. But for one reason or another, plenty of cities are built with a system of canals that gives them their character.

A map of central Amsterdam shows how it's built on a semicircle of concentric canal rings. The medieval city was already encircled by the Singel, which formed a defensive barrier, but

102

as the city grew in the seventeenth century, the city fathers embarked on a town planning experiment to accommodate that growth, using the Singel as the inner belt and adding three more rings - the Herengracht, Prinsengracht and Keizersgracht.

Suzhou, in China, was built on the Grand Canal, a 1,200 mile waterway that ran all the way from Beijing in the north to Hangzhou in the south of the country. In Suzhou, water was used both as a defensive perimeter, and to create beautiful townscapes with waterside teahouses and overhanging trees, but it was the Grand Canal that brought wealth to the city.

When Peter the Great of Russia came to the throne, he decided to make Russia a proper European country. He banned the traditional princely costume, and decided to leave medieval Moscow and build a completely new city on the Baltic Sea. St Petersburg was actually built on a marshland, so creating concentric canals was a good way to deal with water flow - and Peter had spent time in the Netherlands, so no doubt Amsterdam was one of his inspirations.

ON STILTS

Along the banks of the Gironde, in France, there are hundreds of little fishing cabins. Each one of them stands a little way from the bank, on stilts, so that the fishermen can take the small bridge to the cabin and fish into deep water from a convenient and comfortable height.

Building on stilts isn't a new idea. Neolithic and Bronze Age communities were often built on stilts on the edge of a lake, in Austria and Slovenia as well as north Italy; in the Chiloe archipelago of Chile, *palafitos* are still built on stilts along the rocky, steep shore.

There are other reasons for wanting to build on stilts. In Cambodia, for instance, many houses are built on stilts to provide an open, shaded area under the house for use during the day, and protect the living quarters both from floods, and from creepy-crawlies and rodents. Granaries are still put on stilts in many countries where conventional house forms have been adopted - again, stopping the rats from getting in.

And stilt houses are making a real comeback in the age of global warming. There are whole stilt resorts in the Maldives - an entire country whose highest point is just 2.4 meters above sea level - and houses on the Texas coast are now being raised up on stilts to protect against storm damage.

ALL THE FUN OF THE FAIR

THE OLDEST FAIRS IN EUROPE

Fairs in Europe have a very long history. For instance, the Freimarkt in Bremen is now nearly a thousand years old; it started in 1035. It's now the biggest funfair in northern Germany, delivering a fortnight of fun, thrills, and (because this is Germany) beer. Although it started as a trading fair - a free market, in the days of tolls and privileges - the first carousel arrived as early as 1809.

Nottingham Goose Fair is a comparative newcomer, having been started around 1284, and it did originally sell geese as well as other goods. Now, it's one of the UK's biggest fairs, with over 500 rides provided by the Showmen's Guild. Nottingham got its first merry-go-round in 1829, but it was promptly banned by the Council - a false start that the fair has made up for since, with the introduction of gondolas, waltzers, gallopers, bioscopes, and more recently dodgems, roller coasters and a reverse bungee that catapults its customers into the sky. This being England, refreshments include candy floss (cotton candy) and mushy peas.

****** By KlickingKarl - Own work, CC BY-SA 3.0,
https://commons.wikimedia.org/w/index.php?curid=6566545

The fair at Houdan, France, is another venerable institution; it was started by Simon de Montfort in 1065. Unlike Bremen and Nottingham, though, it's remained a small scale fair - there's a fun fair, but the big draw for many locals is the agricultural show which gives pride of place to the mop-headed local 'Houdannais' chickens.

PUSHKAR CAMEL MARKET

Most of the year, Pushkar is a small Indian town, albeit one that does quite well out of Indian pilgrims and western tourists. But once a year, in October or November (the dates move according to the Hindu calendar), it becomes the buzzing, crowded hub of the great camel fair. It's not just camels, some of them beautifully decorated - there's a mustache competition (Rajasthani men take their mustaches very seriously), Marwari horses with their turned-in ears, and lots of wandering holy men who make Pushkar their home for the duration. There's even a horse-dancing competition.

Because Pushkar has a holy lake and a major Brahma temple, a lot of Hindus decide to mix business and religion, and come to the camel fair but also to make their devotions at the temple and bathe in the lake. But there are also big wheels, hot air balloons, and a Wall of Death, as well as the chance to ride in a camel cart around the fairground.

Naturally, touts and shysters of all kinds also flock to the fair. There's a lot of money around - a good Marwari stallion will set you back $10,000 or more and decent camels don't come cheap - and there are people determined to get their hands on some of it. That's the same as any western fair or festival. But there's one very big difference from Bremen Freimarkt or Burning Man - because Pushkar is a holy town, alcohol and drugs are prohibited, as is non-vegetarian food.

SERIOUSLY GREAT MARKETS

Most cities have food markets. Many have craft markets. Some have *great* markets.

For instance the Boqueria food market in Barcelona is a great market. It starts at eight, and by ten in the morning it's completely crowded - though the regulars will already have popped in for their *churros con chocolate* (donuts and hot chocolate) at one of the market's stalls. Fresh seafood, air-dried ham, and local cheeses are just some of the products that make this market a true taste of Spain. (Those wanting to avoid the crowds will find another good market at St Caterina, near the cathedral.)

In Bangkok, Jatujak market is a massive concern that includes a couple of shopping malls as well as an outside market. While parts have become pretty touristy, there are also areas that cater mainly to locals - a pet market, and a whole load of stalls selling various types of packaging, for instance. There are 27 sections and over 15,000 stalls; it's probably a blessing that it's only open at weekends.

The middle east has various great souks -
Dubai's great souk, in Deira, shades
imperceptibly from gold souk to spice souk to
a section selling plastic buckets and cotton
mops. One favorite with many travelers is the
old souk in Muttrah, Oman, where some sweet
stall owners still stir great cauldrons of gloopy
date *halwa* and little mosques open off the souk
streets. Much of it's been refurbished, but the
back streets still have the atmosphere of old
Muttrah.

Singapore has the delightfully named 'hawker
centers', open air food markets that were set up
as a more hygienic alternative to street stalls.
While they have permanent stalls instead of
little wheeled carts, the atmosphere and the
range of food is the same as in the old street
markets - stir fries, noodles, and grills. In Hong
Kong, the Dai Pai Dongs provide great street
food, but here too hawker centers are
beginning to take over.

Bangkok and some other Thai cities have
specific markets given over to the sale of

religious amulets. In Bangkok, it's round Wat Mahathat, one of the most influential Buddhist temples; while stallholders are happy to sell to tourists, most of their trade is with local amulet collectors. The trade appears to combine the nerdy appeal of stamp collecting or train spotting with superstitious reliance on good luck talismans, and it's amusing to see that amulets include not only medallions of Buddhist monks and holy men, but also a range of model penises.

OUTDOORS MARKETS OF SOUTH

AMERICA

In South America, country people still use weekly or bi-weekly markets for many of their needs, and that's particularly true in remote regions such as the Andes. Chichicastenango in Guatemala is one of the most celebrated of the markets; every Thursday and Sunday the entire town is taken over by the market, which sells local handicrafts as well as food, toys, and kitchen utensils. On Sunday, the noise and bustle of the market competes with the religious ceremonies, equally colorful and equally noisy.

Pisac Market in Peru takes place in a picturesque colonial town, villagers trekking in from miles around to sell their produce. Many of them still wear traditional clothing; each village has a slightly different costume. The Sunday market has hundreds of stalls; tourists will head for the local ceramics, silver, or alpaca wool blankets, but should be warned that some of the 'alpaca' is actually polyester. (The difference? Alpaca wool is cooler to the touch, and heavier, than synthetics.)

Buenos Aires is a different kettle of fish. It's a highly developed city and most of its inhabitants would look down their noses at the country bumpkins of Chichi or Pisac. Instead, BA has a Sunday flea market at San Telmo. The Sunday 'feria' isn't just a chance to shop for antiques or look at local crafts; there are street performers (San Telmo is the arty, bohemian quarter of the city), food carts, and guys selling freshly squeezed orange juice.

THE BERBER MARKET OF AZROU,

MOROCCO

Most tourists in Morocco head for the souks of Fez or Marrakesh and buy a pair of leather slippers, or a bit of Berber jewelry. The Berber market in Azrou is a quite different experience. It's not aimed at tourists, for a start; it's part livestock market, part daily essentials shopping, for the folk of the Atlas Mountains, who arrive by pickup or shared taxi, and a few on mules or donkeys. There's a fruit and veg section, and stalls selling yarn for weaving, and electrical goods including spare cables for just about anything.

Buying lunch is something of an experience. There's loads of mint tea - traditionally poured from a great height into a small glass, and made with huge amounts of sugar - and ordering a kebab involves selecting the meat from a huge side of beef hung up in the tent, before it's taken off to be grilled. Wandering fiddle players entertain in the food tents, rewarded by the occasional fistful of small change or, if they're lucky, notes.

And there are also some amazing sights; quack doctors and on-the-spot dentists, or one stand selling second hand sinks, baths, and radiators. Definitely a rather different market from those you'll find in Fez or Marrakesh.

SMITHFIELD MARKET, LONDON

Smithfield Market is one of London's great gems, and is the only one of the great markets still on its original site (the Billingsgate fish market and the Spitalfields and Covent Garden fruit and flower markets have both relocated outside the center of London). It's been there for at least eight hundred years, and quite probably longer.

The market starts at four in the morning and it's all over by midday, when the last of the huge refrigerated lorries leave the streets outside. The splendid Victorian market buildings are still in use every weekday, and are open to the public; indeed most vendors are willing to sell a packet of sausages or a couple of steaks, though their main trade is wholesale.

But the best bargain and the best experience of all is the Christmas Eve auction. Harts butchers auctions the last of its stock before the Christmas holidays - everything has to go, or it will spoil before the market gets back to work in January. Canny locals make sure their freezers are empty before they head to the auction - and they also make sure they have plenty of small value notes and pound coins, because there's no change given.

Best of all the bargains comes at the end of the auction. If there are too many turkeys, customers are invited to toss a coin - if they guess 'heads or tails' correctly, they get their turkey for nothing.

GREAT FLEA MARKETS OF EUROPE

Flea markets are a wonderful way to get to know a country. Different things turn up; in France, for instance, regular finds include beautiful sets of earthenware containers for sugar, coffee, and salt and Le Creuset ironware casseroles, while in England, blue-and-white Wedgwood crockery and Toby Jugs turn up with the occasional pewter tankard for drinking a traditional English pint.

Portugal has two fine flea markets. In Lisbon, the Sunday and Tuesday feira de ladra or 'thieves' market' has a stunning backdrop of tiled house fronts and white church architecture, with a huge range of merchandise including fine earthenware, bookbinders' equipment, and old fountain pens. In the north of the country, Porto also has a huge flea market, where visitors are rather more likely to find unexpected bargains.

Brussels has one of the biggest flea markets, the Jeu de Balle, open every day but with a particularly good spread on weekends. There's everything from antiques to vintage dresses and modern collectibles, an immense variety.

Portobello Road in London is less a flea market than a serious antiques market, though it has different sections - in the arcades, you'll find businesses selling fine antique clocks or Chinese antiquities, while further north, there's a jewelry section, modern arts and crafts, and right at the top, a secondhand market mainly aimed at locals.

Paris has two big *puces* (yes, that means 'fleas'), Saint-Ouen and Vanves. Saint-Ouen has a number of markets spread out over a large area, with some fixed shops and some pavement traders, and a good selection of furniture; Vanves (weekend mornings only) is a pure street market, with a few secondhand stalls at the end closest to the peripherique, and prices are more negotiable. France also has a huge event, the Braderie de Lille, in the autumn, when the entire town of Lille is taken over by a huge flea market. It's crowded, it's tiring, and it's definitely worth a visit.

But as well as the big flea markets, many places have local sales - 'vides greniers' in France, 'car boots' in England, and just 'markets' in Spain. Trawling the local papers or specialist websites for information has become a way of life for many people, and the canny buyer can snap up some fascinating, unique pieces for very little.

CRAWFORD MARKET, MUMBAI

Crawford Market, Mumbai has been officially renamed Mahatma Jyotiba Phule Mandai, but most people will still recognise it as 'Crawford Market' and its Victorian Gothic buildings still deliver a taste of the British Raj. It's a huge, mainly wholesale, food market, open every day except Sunday, and it has become a major tourist attraction. That's led to new traders heading for the market, selling souvenirs as well as dried and fresh food.

Around Crawford market, there's a massive wholesale district. Buying a pen and a notebook is impossible; buying ten pens and 24 notebooks? No problem! Different areas offer textiles, stationery, household goods, and even pets, often at bargain prices - though buyers may need to haggle.

GREAT MODERN

ARCHITECTURE

A DRIVERLESS TRAIN TOUR OF

DOCKLANDS

Docklands is the result of a Thatcherite vision - a massive development zone that threw away the planning rulebook. Glass and chrome skyscrapers, 'Lego' houses, even pumping stations with ancient Egyptian details, anything could happen here, in the huge wastelands left when the Port of London moved out.

Almost all the old warehouses have gone (a few still survive in Wapping and two house the Museum of Docklands), but the port left behind huge expanses of water, which give the area its character. Skyscrapers are reflected in the water, and the large basins balance out the vertical thrust of the buildings.

Some of the architecture, particularly in the central Canary Wharf development, is very 1980s glitz and glamor, but there are more understated sights, too - small Scandinavian-inspired houses with wooden cladding, and China Wharf with its bright red walls and semi-circular 'eyebrow' windows.

Best of all, though, is the transport system. While Canary Wharf was all about flashing the cash, London Transport decided a real tube line would be too expensive. Instead, it built the ridiculously cheap Docklands Light Railway, whose stubby little driverless trains give one of the best views of the area's modern architecture - often from bridges high above the water.

La Defense, Paris

La Defense's iconic building is the Grande Arche, a minimalist echo of the Arc de Triomphe. It's a very French concept, completing the *axe historique* which starts at the Louvre and runs in a dead straight line along the Champs Elysées, past the Arc de Triomphe and along the Avenue de la Grande Armée.

It gives the impression of a highly worked out master plan. In fact, La Defense took much longer to develop than London's Docklands; the first high-rise office buildings here were erected in the 1950s and 1960s. By the 1980s, La Defense had a cluster of cheap high-rise developments, but no defining feature; it wasn't till President Mitterand stepped in that the Grande Arche project was conceived to create a symbol of the French nation on a massive scale.

New towers are still being built for this thriving business district. But it's also become a major tourist attraction with 8 million visitors a year, who come to see the Grande Arche reflected in its fountains, or to climb to the skydeck on the roof for a marvelous view of Paris.

GARDENS IN THE SKY

The idea of gardens in the sky is a lovely one but it doesn't always work. Plans for a full-grown forest in the top of London's 'Walkie Talkie' skyscraper looked beautiful, but the reality was dismissed by one architectural critic as looking more like a cross between a Center Parcs holiday camp and an airport terminal. The Coulée Verte in Paris and the High Line in New York work better - old elevated sections of railway that have been remade as linear gardens - but they're intimate rather than spectacular experiences.

However, things are changing, partly as a result of concern over global warming. While vertical gardens started out on high-profile buildings like hotels and corporate headquarters, the movement is broadening out. In Milan, two high-rise residential developments have been created featuring lush gardens and even fully grown trees on their specially reinforced balconies.

But it's Singapore which has staked a claim to leadership with its Gardens by the Bay. This public garden combines the appeal of a normal park - lush plantings and meandering paths - with vertical gardens in 18 huge 'supertrees'. Best of all, there's a walkway 25 meters above the ground which lets visitors walk among the supertrees and experience them from close up. At night, the solar-powered trees light up, and the gardens are open till two in the morning. A wonder of the modern world!

NATURE IN A BUILDING

Modern architecture has mainly been rectilinear, sharp, and defiantly 'man made', with materials like concrete, chrome, and glass. But there's always been a counterculture fight-back, with natural materials and soft outlines that reflect natural forms.

The 'peanut' gridshell at the Weald & Downland museum in Sussex, England, is one of these, and its warm and slightly comic character has won it many friends. Among many old vernacular buildings, it remains defiantly modern but its oak lath structure fits well with the half-timbered houses of the past.

The Republic of Georgia has a fantastic tradition of modern architecture; since it split from the USSR it's sponsored some amazing work, including a turf-roofed police station like a melted flying saucer in Mtskheta, and a performing arts venue in Tbilisi that looks like a giant slinky. There's even a police station that looks like a cross between Chinese calligraphy and a climbing wall in the mountain resort of Mestia.

Andrea   Kirkby   on   flickr;
https://www.flickr.com/photos/andreakirkb
y/39922773811

Iraqi-British architect Zaha Hadid started off
with quite stark, linear buildings, but ended up
creating buildings whose irregular curves and
crannies reflect the work of nature. Her
Dondaemun Design Plaza, in Seoul, Korea,
undulates like a giant wave, and includes a
walkable park on the roof; in Hong Kong, her

Jockey Club Innovation tower rises like a flame or a rocky headland; and her Havenhuis port building in Antwerp, Belgium, has what looks like a huge boulder - or perhaps a streamlined boat - balanced on top of the older, classical building.

Frank Gehry combines both strands of architecture, notably in his Guggenheim Museum, Bilbao, Spain, with its swooping wave forms and undulating glass and titanium panels. As soon as it was topped out it was recognized as a masterpiece of modern architecture. Smaller, but equally stunning, is his BP Pedestrian bridge in Chicago, which wriggles like a giant metallic snake across Columbus Drive to connect two green parks.

FROM THE KITSCH TO THE SUBLIME

Everything is bigger in Texas, they say - but that saying has become rather dated. The real place that everything is bigger is now Dubai, which with Burj Khalifa houses the tallest building in the world. Burj Khalifa is a stunning, slender building which rises from a buttressed, almost pyramidal base to a glass spire at the top.

Dubai's modern architecture is sometimes sublime. Just as often it's remarkably kitsch. The Atlantis hotel on The Palm has a huge Arab-style arch in the center of its facade, a dozen stories high. But if that makes it sound like the minimalist Grande Arche de la Defense, think again; it's a Las Vegas style vision of Arabia, with little pavilioned turrets on top of what's actually a rather banal building. The Raffles Hotel goes even further in ancient references with its grand pyramid design, complete with a winking light at the apex; tasteful it isn't. There's even a whole 'traditional' Arab souk where visitors can shop beside a Venetian canal.

Far more interesting (and far more like the Grande Arche) is the DIFC Gate, a massive gray stone cube with one open side, and a criss-cross frieze of glass instead of a cornice. There's the Burj Al-Arab, a luxury hotel built in the form of a sail, and the wave-like Jumeirah Beach hotel, a real oldster in Dubai terms having been built in 1997.

For more than twenty years Dubai has been an architects' playground. While credit crunches clipped its wings for a few years - several of the planned artificial reef communities are now slowly sliding back into the sea - it's never lost the building fever, and new towers are still going up. A compulsory visit for any fan of modern architecture.

A MACHINE FOR WORSHIPING IN

Le Corbusier famously said a house was just 'a machine for living in', which would make his chapel at Ronchamp, France a machine for worshiping in. Though the architect's trademark concrete and simple outlines are very much in evidence, it's a more poetic work than that would suggest. From the outside, its sweeping roofs suggest a nun's wimple or a wave form, while the interior features jewel-like stained glass.

Le Corbusier also built an entire city, Chandigarh, in India. As so often, he used raw concrete as his main building material, and he incorporated the local landscape into his design. He also used sunlight and shadow to create strong sculptural highlights. While Chandigarh has grown since Le Corbusier built its central portion, it's kept to his grid, and it's still one of the most pedestrian-friendly and humane city centers in India.

YOU DON'T HAVE TO BE CRAZY TO MAKE

ARCHITECTURE, BUT IT HELPS

Friedensreich Hundertwasser wasn't actually insane, but he was a pretty crazy architect. He opposed standardisation and mass production, and he hated straight lines - which put him in opposition to Modernism, Post-Modernism, and pretty much all contemporary architecture. He even called straight lines "godless and immoral". Instead, he designed pictorial architecture that used collage, bright color, and organic forms to create immensely lively buildings.

Perhaps his craziest and cutest building is in Kawakawa, New Zealand, where he lived for many years. It has wavy lines, mosaic tiles, and even a tree growing out of the architecture. And unlike most prestige projects, which are arts centers, banks, government buildings, or opera houses, this building has a more humble but very necessary purpose - it's a public toilet.

WONDERFUL BRIDGES

A bridge, for some people, is just a way from A to B. These are the kind of people who criticized the lovely Millennium Bridge in London because it 'wobbled'.

But bridges are about much, more more. They're architectural statements in their own right. Which is why the Millau Viaduct in France is so amazing. Not only is it the tallest bridge in the world, crossing the deep Tarn valley, but its slender supporting pillars make it a real beauty.

Newcastle, England, has a remarkable array of bridges crossing the river Tyne. The latest is the Millennium Bridge, the world's only tilting bridge; it was designed so that the semicircular walkway can tilt upwards to let ships pass underneath, and looks like a winking eye. It's a remarkable innovation.

The Romans knew all about infrastructure, and they also knew how to make a political statement about the superiority of the Roman empire. The Pont du Gard near Nimes, in France, takes an aqueduct across the Gardon river on no fewer than three arcades, its arches soaring high above the valley floor. At Merida, in Spain, the 'miracle' aqueduct is 25 meters high, again with three tiers of arches, and still impresses even though it's now incomplete. In Roman times Merida had two other aqueducts, and water was brought from more than 15 kilometers away.

THE SHARK TANK

The insurance firm Willis Faber and Dumas commissioned a new headquarters back in the 1960s, and got an uncompromising modern design from Norman Foster and Wendy Cheesman. From the outside, it's a sheer wall of black glass, curving to make the most of the oddly shaped site; above, though, a green garden covers much of the roof, visible only from the sky.

It's rather a success, because despite its defiant modernity, it's quite unassuming; the black glass reflects its surroundings, including the classical Unitarian Meeting House and other seventeenth and eighteenth century buildings.

But of course, because it's home to an insurance firm, and its similarity to an aquarium was quickly noticed, in very short order it acquired the sobriquet of 'the shark tank'.

ALTERNATIVES

The 'bucket list' is an ugly phenomenon. '1000 places to visit before you die' (when else would you visit? - unless of course you're German - see under 'corpse tourism' above!) has pushed even more people towards overcrowded tourist sights like Angkor Wat, Macchu Picchu, the Taj Mahal and the Great Pyramids.

Of course Angkor Wat is worth seeing. Of course the Taj is wonderful. But if you want to avoid the crowds, there are great alternatives that are very nearly as good - and without the tourist hustle and bustle.

ANGKOR WAT - PREAH VIHEAR

The Khmer kings didn't just build at Angkor. This temple, far in the north of Cambodia, was built on a hilltop ridge, with a huge paved causeway leading up to the top temple. It has refined architecture, it has beautifully carved

138

lintels, and it has views extending for miles over the Cambodian plains - something you don't get at Angkor. It also has very few western tourists, and - because it's on the Thai border - sandbagged gun emplacements along with some friendly English-speaking soldiers. Altogether a different visit from the crowded and expensive Angkor.

TAJ MAHAL - SIKANDRA

The Taj Mahal is India's top tourist sight - it's practically synonymous with India in most people's minds. But it's incredibly crowded; at peak times it's like the Tokyo Metro inside the mausoleum as tourists push and shuffle round the tombs of Shah Jahan and his beloved Mumtaz Mahal.

At Sikandra, the Emperor Akbar's mausoleum is a much less well known sight, visited mainly by Indian courting couples who wander the gardens outside to see the tame antelopes and friendly squirrels. It's a massive building, with charming little pavilions on top, and an ornate flower decorated mosaic inside, and there's always a stick of incense burning on Akbar's tomb. The Taj is elegant, but Sikandra is massive and solemn, a quite different strand of Mughal architecture.

Andrea Kirkby on flickr: https://www.flickr.com/photos/andreakirkby/9428627340

Another alternative is the 'baby Taj' at Aurangabad, properly known as the Bibi ka Maqbara. It looks very like the Taj from the outside, but the inside has a spectacular surprise; a huge opening in the floor lets visitors gaze down on the tombs in the basement story. Many throw rose petals or coins down on to the tomb of Dilras Banu Begum, wife of the emperor Aurangzeb.

THE PARTHENON - TEMPLES OF PAESTUM

The Parthenon in Athens is a wonderful sight, commanding the city from the very top of the Acropolis rock, and surrounded by ancient buildings like the Erechtheion and the huge monumental gate. But it's disastrously crowded. And it's still a building site - repair works are ongoing, so parts may be covered in scaffolding.

Strangely, its best rival for top Greek temple is in Italy. The temples of Paestum were erected by Greek colonists who had decided the fertile soil of southern Italy would make them wealthier than the dry, rocky slopes of their homeland; the Romans called this area 'Magna Graecia', big Greece. At Paestum, there's not one temple but three, now surrounded by green lawns; they're in a more archaic style than the Parthenon, and they never had the beautiful sculptures of the Parthenon. (But then, those sculptures are currently in the British Museum, so the Parthenon has no advantage these days.)

PYRAMIDS AND PYRAMIDS

The great pyramids of Giza are one of the seven wonders of the ancient world, and nowadays incredibly popular with tourists. There's a whole industry of camel rides and tourist tat that's grown up around them.

Far away from the tourist hot-spots of Cairo, the pyramids of Meroe are still marooned in sand. They were built by the Kushite dynasty of pharaohs, who became the 25th Dynasty of ancient Egypt, and they are real pyramids - though slightly different from the Giza model, with smaller footprints but a steeper slope. They're quite uncrowded, though they're difficult to get to, about 3 hours' drive from Khartoum, the capital of Sudan.

A TALE OF TWO CITIES - A TALE OF FOUR

CHURCHES

Westminster Abbey costs £16 to visit, and is always full of tourists. Notre Dame de Paris costs nothing (unless you want to go up the towers) but it's equally choc-a-bloc with visitors.

However, just up the road from Westminster Abbey is Westminster Cathedral. It's not a medieval building and it doesn't have a Poets' Corner, but it is a splendid work, a huge neo-Byzantine basilica with a remarkable bell tower and splendid marble pavements and mosaics. Definitely worth a visit - perhaps not as an alternative to the Abbey but as an addition.

In Paris, the abbey of Saint Denis is a few metro stops from Notre Dame and is in many ways more interesting. Notre Dame's monuments were quite extensively cleared out during the Revolution; Saint Denis, on the other hand, actually acquired more, since some of the royal tombs that had once been housed in other abbeys were brought to the collection here. This abbey was the first Gothic building in France, houses a huge collection of royal tombs, and some remarkable stained glass, and it never seems to be particularly busy. A definite plus, some of the local couscous restaurants are magnificent.

MACHU PICCHU - CHOQUEQUIRAO

While Choquequirao isn't any easier to spell than Machu Picchu, it has various other advantages. It's a two-day hike from Cuzco, though at some point there are plans for a cable car that will reduce it to fifteen minutes.

Like Machu Picchu, Choquequirao has a picturesque site on a mountain ridge, and terraces of stone buildings. It also has rather sweet pictographs of llamas marked out on some of its terraces in lighter colored stones set in the wall. Visitors will need to take their own camping equipment, but at least they'll be able to enjoy the sunrise on their own, or with the select company of a few other seasoned hikers.

VENICE - CHIOGGIA

'La Serenissima' is no longer serene - the city council has even introduced barriers on some of the main thoroughfares to try to stem the flow of tourists. While Venice's great history and attractions such as the San Marco basilica with its rich mosaics can't be replaced, a flavor of the Venetian canals and architecture is accessible without the crowds in nearby Chioggia.

There are no gondolas, but little boats still tie up inside the city, and fresh seafood comes in daily thanks to the fishermen of the little port. The historic center is like Venice shrunk to a village, with its cathedral, white marble bridge, and with the relaxed feel of a small town that hasn't changed a lot since the 1950s.

A PURRFECT WAY TO SEE

THE WORLD

Cat cafes have spread through the world now - there are cafes in Lviv, St Petersburg, Paris, Montreal, Singapore, Budapest and even Chiang Mai, Thailand. But there are other places ailurophiles should definitely visit.

THE WORLD'S FIRST CAT CAFE

Although the cat cafe really took off in Japan, it's Taiwan that invented the phenomenon; Taipei claims to have the world's first ever cat cafe, Cafe Dogs & Cats 1998 - originally named Cat Flower Garden. Tokyo didn't get one till 2005.

Taiwan now has a whole cat village, Houtong, where every business has at least a couple of house cats, and many have cat memorabilia displayed. Apparently, it all happened by accident - a photographer shot some pictures of cats in the village which went viral, and next thing the villagers knew, cats were bing abandoned here. Soft-hearted, and not all that wealthy, the locals looked for a way to feed the new arrivals - and hey presto! Cat village was born.

THE BOOK MARKET, ISTANBUL

Sahaflar Carsisi, in Istanbul, is a compulsory stop for cat lovers. Not because of the books, and not because of the beautiful Beyazit Mosque that stands next door - but because one stall holder is a cat lover. His stall usually has at least one or two cats exploring the shelves, and one curled up on his chair - and he has built a special drinking fountain for his feline companions.

THE ISLANDS OF CATS

Japan has not one, not three, but twelve different 'cat islands'.

Aoshima is the most famous, with cats outnumbering the human population of the island by at least six to one. The cats all descend from ships' cats who jumped ship, or got left behind, and they have a good life, being fed by the residents every day.

On Tashiro-jima island, the cats were introduced to help keep down the mice and protect the silkworms on which islanders depended for their living. The locals have now banned dogs from the island, and have even erected a cat temple.

These islands are off the tourist track, but Enoshima is easier to get to; it's south-west of Tokyo, and has views of Mount Fuji. In summer, surfers and swimmers throng the beaches, but the cats prefer to laze on doorsteps or on the grass behind the seafront.

Other cat islands include Okishima, in the middle of Lake Biwa; Sanagishima, in the Inland Sea; Muzukijima, where cats patrol the citrus groves; Manabeshima, Iwaishima, Genkaishima, Kadarashima, Aijima and Aishima.

While almost all these communities were started by populations of working cats that were supposed to make themselves useful, the cats have managed to win over the local population and now have a wonderful life, protected by their human servants.

HELLO KITTY!

Hello Kitty is an incredibly popular cartoon character, a little white cat with a red bow in her hair. She's very, very cute, and she even has theme parks devoted to her.

Sanrio Puraland in Tama, Japan is the original theme park dedicated to all the Sanrio characters, not just Hello Kitty but her friends like Little Twin Stars and Hummingmint. There's another Hello Kitty park in Zhejiang, China, which opened in 2015, and the Museum of Contemporary Art held a Hello Kitty Convention in 2014. There are Hello Kitty food trucks all over, and in Johor, Malaysia, there's a Hello Kitty town and even a Hello Kitty hotel.

You can even take a flight with Eva Air from Taipei to Taipei to destinations including Tokyo, Singapore and LA on a Hello Kitty pink plane - or take the Shinkansen bullet train on the West Japan line, which has Hello Kitty livery, pink ribbons and bows, and even plays the Hello Kitty theme tune when it arrives at a station.

THE CAT TEMPLES OF BEKKALALE

India has some very odd temples - temples to movie stars, to politicians, and to snakes - so perhaps it's not surprising that it also has a cat temple. The little village of Bekkalale has no fewer than three temples devoted to the goddess Mangamma in the form of a cat. (Since the god Vishnu managed to appear as a fish, a turtle, a boar, a lion, and a dwarf, a cat avatar isn't really pushing the boat out.)

The villagers see Mangamma as the protector of their village; no one's allowed to kick or hit a cat, and if anyone finds a dead cat, it must be honorably interred.

It's probably quite a good thing that Bekkalale is in south India, a long way from Rajasthan. Who know what would happen if the

Bekkalale cats found out that the Karni Mata temple in Bikaner is full of rats - 25,000 of them? There'd be war among the gods!

HEMINGWAY'S POLYDACTYL CATS

One of the strangest attractions of Key West is a population of polydactyl cats - felines with an extra toe on each paw. A sea captain gave writer Ernest Hemingway a kitten called Snow White (sailors, apparently, thought the extra toe brought luck) and about 60 of her descendants now roam the grounds of the Hemingway Museum on Key West.

Not all polydactyl cats are equal, though; some have six toes on their front paws, instead of the normal five, but others have seven.

CAT MUSEUMS

Believe it or not there are several cat museums in the world. In North Carolina, a retired biology professor created the American Museum of the House Cat, alongside a cat shelter, which has rescued over 3,000 felines. Some of the exhibits might not appeal to every cat lover, though - one is a mummified cat that was found in a house wall in England, walled up probably as some kind of witchcraft.

Singapore's cat museum, unfortunately, has closed, since its lease expired - a real pity since like the North Carolina museum its remit extended to finding new homes for abandoned felines. But there's a rather nice cat museum in Essex Place, Cincinnati, Ohio. It's a bit different, too, since it's devoted to one very special kind of cat - the Japanese Lucky Cat, the little chap you'll find in most Japanese and many Chinese restaurants waving one paw up and down to welcome you.

The problem with cats, of course, if that if not neutered, they can reproduce very quickly. The owners of the Cincinatti museum found that out the hard way. One little 'Maneki neko', as the lucky cats are called, led to enough cats to fill a bookcase, and then a whole room - and eventually, to a small museum, which opens during the Essex ArtWalks seasons.

THE CATS OF YORK

The city of York promises many magnificent sights; the Gothic Minster church, the Merchant Adventurers' Hall, the old Shambles where butchers used to trade and half-timbered houses hang across the road. But one of the most intriguing sights is that of the cats.

First you see one - walking along a window ledge, high up, or silhouetted on the ridge of a roof. Then another, crouched to spring from a balcony. The little statues are scattered throughout the city center. Two of them go

156

back over a century, but the others were commissioned from a local sculptor by architect Tom Adams, who used them as his signature on buildings he'd designed.

Now, York Lucky Cats, a glass shop, has leaflets letting visitors follow the lucky cat trail. And houses with a lucky cat on the roof sell for a premium, according to York estate agents.

MUMMIFIED CATS OF EGYPT

Everyone knows that the ancient Egyptians worshiped cats - and as comic novelist Terry Pratchett said, the cats haven't forgotten.

They also mummified cats. Since they mummified people to give them eternal life, why not let cats have a chance too? And since there were huge numbers of cats - they were protected from maltreatment, and even mollycoddled, by the Egyptians - there are huge numbers of cat mummies. Some are enclosed in beautiful little sarcophagi, as well as in their layers of wrappings; others have their linen wrappings painted with pretty designs. There are cat mummies in the Louvre, the British Museum, the Met, and other museums round the world.

Some estimates show the number of mummified cats could be as high as 80 million. Since possessing a mummified cat was lucky, there was some cheating going on; one mummy was unwrapped only to show it contained a single cat bone among a lot of packing, while another was entirely made of mud. One cat had been packed with a kitten next to it to make it look bigger (and probably more expensive).

And sad to say, some of the cats probably weren't cosseted - they were murdered, by a cat-mummifier with a quota to meet.

CAT CITY

Kuching, Malaysia, is Catsville Arizona, so to speak - its very name means 'cat' in Malay. Cats are celebrated everywhere in the town.

There are giant statues of cats at road intersections. Cats are painted on walls; there's a cat fountain, and cats even appear on the city's crest. Even the local radio station is CAT FM. In the town hall, a giant cat opens its jaws to provide a doorway to the little cat museum.

And yes, Kuching has a cat cafe.

A TINY TEMPLE JUST FOR CATS

Most people just walk past it. It's a tiny temple, not much bigger than the little 'spirit house' that every Thai family has in the back garden. It's just off the pavement on Phra Athit Road, just a few blocks away from the backpacker district of the Khao San Road, its seedy hotels and noisy nightclubs. A few takeaway containers lie untidily at the foot of the shrine.

Stop and read the sign, though, and you find out it's a little cat temple. Not a temple to a cat, but for cats. Local restaurateurs bring odds and ends and leftovers for the cats, and an offering box collects small change to help pay their vet's bills. Besides, the ledges by the temple provide a great place for the cats to lounge - or wait for their next meal.

Thais seem to take good care of their cats, with many Buddhist temples also having as many feline occupants as monks - and many Buddhists donating food as part of their charitable effort, or to 'gain merit' in another life.

BUDDHIST CATS

More Buddhist cats are to be found in Tokyo, where the Gotokuji and Imado temples house large numbers of the little beasts - though not real ones, but cat models given as offerings.

At Gotokuji, the regular offering is the maneki neko, the little nodding cat - the shrine is surrounded by huge numbers of statues, in different sizes but all of them in white and orange, and raising their right paw in welcome. Around the temple, street artists have got into the act with cat art on walls and posters.

There are a number of stories about samurai who were saved from storms or falling trees by little cats who waved their paws to beckon them away from danger; whatever the truth of the tales, people who have enjoyed good luck offer a maneki neko here to say thanks. If they have an unfulfilled desire, they buy a painted board instead; on the front, there's a Buddha and a beckoning cat, and on the back, they write what they want to pray for.

Cutest note of all; the temple bell is made in the form of a cat's collar bell.

At Imado shrine, two lucky cats sit on the altar, and the cats are almost always in couples. Even the watering cans in the garden are in the shape of cats, with their curly tails making the handle and spout. Although Imado isn't as well known as Gotokuji, it's thought that this is where the maneki neko originated - a local potter made the first one, and it all took off from there.

Thanks for your purchase.

We also recommend that you get

"Surprising and Shocking Fun Facts:
The Treasure Book of Amazing Trivia"
by to compliment this book.

You can purchase it on this Link:
https://www.amazon.com/dp/B07D6
QJ7H1

Made in the USA
Lexington, KY
05 March 2019